SENSITIZED SOUL

FOR A BETTER SOCIETY

KONDA MURALI

I dedicate this book to all the people who always think about the society and want to bring some change on behalf of them. As a son to parents, as a brother and as a husband, we fulfil our duties to the fullest to our family. Apart from fulfilling our duties to the family, we should be accountable to the society, then only, we can expect some change.

I also dedicate this book to myself as I fulfil the duties of the family and the duties of the society as a son and parent and a teacher and a writer.

Contents

Contents

Contents

Contents

Contents

Foreword

I am very happy to write foreword of the book, Sensitized Soul- For a better society by Konda Murali. After reading the book, I felt the poet wants convey his instinct inclination to change the society. Every poem in the book vividly depicts the different problems faced by the society. All the poems are simple to understand and they are written with good rhythm and prosaic elements. Overall the book is simply super. This book will definitely enlighhten the readers and create good reading experience.

Sabitha Indra Reddy
Education Minister
Telangana State

Acknowledgements

I would like to acknowlwdge this book to Smt. Sabitha Indra Reddy, Education Minister, Telangana State for encouraging me to write the books. I will never forget the motivation she instilled in me.

Preface

After witnessing several incidents in the world, my heart is sensitized. One of such incidents is the Russian and Ukraine war. Everybody knows that this is an age of technology. The man has developed in all apsects and changed the world. Nobody guessed that the wars occur in the developed world. On the contrary, Russia invaded Ukraine for some reasons. After seeing the terrific attack, i felt that the movie fight scene are some better. In this way, it is composed 101 lucid, vivid poems, taking some social evils. It is also presented how human's beahviour towards his society has changed. The book depicts what one can do to change the society from their part. The poems composed on the several topics like philosophy, love, life, political parties' policies and about the great personalities.

Prologue

Konda Murali is an author and poet of 14 best selling books. Apart from writing books, he works as a PGT English in Telangana Minorities Residential School at Jangaon.

His books list:

1. Bittersweet Juices
2. A book on English Literary Terms
3. Forget and Forgive
4. The Racharla Fort
5. The Pearls of Life
6. The Profound Emotions
7. Lockdown Stories
8. The Real Dreams
9. Love and Life
10. Balakanda
11. Aranyakanda
12. Thrilling Telangana
13. Sita's abduction
14. Sensitized Soul

1. Our Kashmir

Kashmir is an integral part of India
The issue was brought in world media
About this issue, the world had no idea
Pakistan illegally occupied the area

India had the ability to handle the issue
Now one can notice, how is India's view?
At international level, know India's value
The country's respect in the world grew

The government removed 370 article
With the article, Kashmir itself can rule
It can protect the rights of fundamental
Now everything there is constitutional

2. Indian Flag

National flag is a symbol of free country
National flag of India has a grand history
The flag is in horizontal with tricoloured
Saffron, white and green are equally fixed

Navy blue wheel represents life and death
Saffron stands for the nation's strength
White indicates righteousness and truth
Green shows the country's fertility, growth

The Indian flag may be hoisted anywhere
The citizens are inspired by flag's flutter
The flag makes the Indians to feel pride
The flag awakes patriotism countrywide

3. A leader of humanism

Martin Luther King was a leader of civil rights
He followed Gandhi's activism of nonviolence
He led marches for right to vote and labour rights
His speech, "I have a dream" became very famous

Martin Luther was awarded Nobel prize for peace
He also fought against poverty and the wars
He faced many hurdles to establish peace in US
He proved that nonviolence only brings peace

I don't know why good samaritans are assassinated
Like this, few episodes in the history is exemplified
Gandhi, Lincoln, Kennedy, Indira were assassinated
From this, Martin Luther King was not exempted

4. A lengend

Babu Jagjivan Ram was an Indian statesman
He was instrumental leader and spokesman
Jagjivan Ram dedicated his whole life for strife
He was an Indian leader, tried to keep India safe

Babuji strived to get independence for the country
After getting freedom, he fought for equality
He also fought for rights of Dalits in assembly
That is why, Babuji was called as the revolutionary

People are born and they die, developing themselves
Legendaries are born and they live for others
Living for oneself is not the actual cause of birth
Living for others get them success, no death

5. Pule-Demi god

Some people are born to develop themselves
Some people are born to develop their societies
Jyothiba's birth filled light in the ages of darkness
His birth freed the sackles of Indian old customs

Jyothibha Pule is the demi god for lower communities
Mahatma stood first to fight for the social justice
Pule was the man who put his ideas into practice
Pule was the leader who didn't wait the followers

Leaders bear negativity to impart fruits to others
Pule bore the hurdles to keep society with happiness
Some people die and be forgotten with the times
Some people live eternally even after their demise

6. God and Demi god

The name, Ambedkar is so popular
Babasaheb is only the true secular
To the constitution, he is the father
Simply, he was a great philosopher

B.R.Ambedkar is a god to the dalits
He is a demigod to all the Indians
He is the encyclopedia to lawyers
He is a critic of orthodox religions

I've no adequate words to describe
His knowledge on society is superb
Drafting constitution has no diatribe
Ambedkar's life is inspiring in globe

7. Half of the sky

Women are caretakers and contributors
They are educators and entrepreneurs
They are also politicians and peasants
And they are employees and entertainers

Women plan meal program for a family
Thus they also plan economy for a country
They are longterm developers of a territory
They are finally extraordinary, revolutionary

Women are half of the sky and the earth
They are family's and country's strength
Biologically weak but mind power is mammoth
They are the reason for health and wealth

Women are the creators of human race
And they are preservers of the populace

So we allow them for all and not cease
They are the best, this we must notice

8. Gender Equality

Gender equality should start from home
Then the changeover will be awesome
In doing work, boys shouldn't feel irksome
Home work is women's work, they assume

Gender equality itself shouldn't be biased
It is not women's problem, understand?
Men's hidden problem has to be noticed
Equality should be in quality, not in limited

In fact, both women and men are different
Like variety species of vegetable and fruit
No two races are same, in the sense of vast
But it is not men, women, it is human sort

9. A Social Reformer

Kanshiram was a social reformer
He was a charismatic people's leader
He tried to build confidence in dalits
And he uplifted the backward classes

He founded the Bahujan Samaj Party
He blessed his protégé Mayavathi
His agenda was to make dalits leaders
He also tried curb communal riots

Kanshiram converted into Budhism
as it taught humanism not religionism
He wrote many books for dalit leaders
His legacy in Uttar Pradesh is continous

10. People's qualities

In Satya Yuga, the people were very righteous
In dwapara Yuga, the people were very desirous
In Treta Yuga, the people were with conscientious
In Kali Yuga, the people were with full of quarrels

The cyber age taught people to do crimes on computers
The people's qualities were changing with the times
But the flattery is steady and stable in the all ages
"The age of flattery" is the amalgamation of all qualities

In this age, it is indefinite to judge the people
The word, hypocrisy itself is not at all suitable
An ability to know good and bad will be unsuccessful
Chaos, conflict, clash and confusion will prevail

11. Jai Jawan

We wonder what the soldiers do
We believe their life is luxurious
Their life is happy, it is a dejavu
They are deployed at the borders

Their life is horrible in cold climate
There, they lack basic amenities
The eateries are without the taste
They always try for nation's peace

The soldiers regulate emergencies
They strictly follow stringent rules
They should combat at anytime
So their life is sorrow, not charm

12. Rights and Duties

The rights give freedom to politics
The parliament prevents dictators
Courts poke nose in irrational acts
So the rights have the limitations

Besides the rights, there are duties
Duties recall our societal behaviors
It is exactly like take and give policy
Society gives us, payback to society

All this chaos is to establish peace
Peace makes the hut as the palace
Without peace, there is no integrity
So abiding to the law is exemplary

13. Jai Hind

Nethaji was a freedom fighter
He started, "Free India Center"
His jingoism made him hero
Bose had his own manifesto

He was against to discussions
Believed in the wars and fights
Did his best to Indian Congress
Strived for Indian independence

His popular slogan was "Jai Hind"
It filled spirit in Hind and Sindh
He was an unprecedented leader
His bravery is identified forever

14. Walk of snail

Walk of the snail is so better than
the acts made by the governments
People change with the situation
The acts change with the elections

From time of diarchy to democracy,
the people saw many types of rules
From age of patriarchy to Plutocracy
medicine is same in different bottles

From British rule to Bharath's rule
the problems grew like a law book
Acts act according to autocrat's will
No one knows a layman's setback

15. Glory In Real Life

GIRL means Glory In Real Life
She is mother, sister and wife
We know, now she is unsafe
So shouldn't get into mischeif
Girl is not burden to the family
She is their invaluable property
She is in the form of humanity
Society should know this reality
Girl brings happiness and joy
She is not less than any boy
Don't treat her as if she is a toy
Let her live the life and enjoy

16. Our responsibilities

They are like invalid cheques in the banks
They are forgotten newyear resolutions
They are the dirts in decorated dust bin
They are inedible cuisines in the function

We change our vote prices, every election
We encourage politicians to trade & earn
We ask our parents' incapable upbringing
We forget looking after at age of declining

We can ask what a society should give us
We should answer to its set of questions
When we are born, we get few innate rights
After growing we will get few innate duties

Chapter17

Why do you bother about the female?
It isn't good to think about her makeup
With makeup, she tries to be powerful
You should make your mind so sharp

It is wrong, "We should empower them"
Let her grow in the way what she wants
Who're we to let her to live with solemn?
Let her raise voice and take her decisions

Don't worry about her wealth & welfare
She is the best unrecognized economist
And she is the perfect untrained doctor
Only thing we do is don't take it to heart

18. A successful person

You will be a successful person
if someone starts imitating you.
Imitation may be your creation
or your notion, they pursue you.

They may feel jealous of you,
for having invincible qualities.
The irrefutable attitude of you
makes them feel stupendous.

Money, power and education
may not make man the model.
Reading people with perfection
can stand a man as exceptional

19. A sign of spring

Vasantha Panchami is a sign of spring
Saraswathi is the godess of learning
The spring season is very fascinating
The festival is a day of thanksgiving

Money and health may have a downfall
Education is indestructible, perennial
The true wealth is knowledge and skill
All these, Vasantha Panchami will recall

Study transforms from darkness to light
Spring tells us to think, hope for the best
Srong man who is an idiot is less violent
Man with half knowledge has no benefit

20. A symbol of humanism

To transform people, god faced problem
But a man tried his best in the kaliyugam
He had devoted his life for vaishnavam
The man always had thirst for wisdom

Ramanujacharya was a man of glorious
His life is an inspiration to the societies
He let everyone to learn vedas, puranas
In those days, he changed old customs

He faced many hurdles to get kaivalyam
He ran after the gurus with enthusiasm
He was form of the god in the kaliyugam
Ramanujacharya is a symbol of humanism

21. God is not in mantras

We shouldn't see the god in matras
See the god in the hearts of humans
The kind think about the welfare of us
But their goodness becomes curse

Everyone will have their own beliefs
It will not always be good to oppose
Just we need, is "A bit of tolerance"
Acceptance attitude appeases us

A little ego leads to many problems
Dropping ego gets lot of happiness
Worshipping god is in many forms
One should follow these principles

22. Blasphemy became a fashion

Don't try to highlight by abusing someone
Everyone can tell what the problems are
Few people come up with proper solution
It is so better to avoid such men of straw

These days, blasphemy became a fashion
After reading, do not come to an opinion
Books are always not a source of cognition
Internal entity tells what you have done

Believe in your religion but respect others'
Prattling publicly, one cannot get results
You believe in Ravana, no one contradicts
But don't blame Rama, he is god to others

23. A soul soother

India lost another popular voice
She brought life to her songs
Bharath Ratna is so prestigious
But she got it with utmost ease

Commonly heros have the fans
Lata Mangeshkar has devotees
She stood top among the singers
Her voice suited many heroines

From an eavesdropper to a singer
her journey was like never before
To the family, she is a bread winner
To the country, she is soul soother

24. An influential media

Social media is an influential media
For people, commenting on it is trivia
People behave as if they have hysteria
No one is careful and has no phobia

Liking, loving and mainly commenting
To them, the media is very interesting
If they hurt others, it will be appalling
If unluck favors, they will be disappointing

A simple comment may hurt a person
a religion, a region, surprisingly a nation
A tweet of Hyundai, a company of Korean
created strong displeasure in the nation

25. True leadership

Leadership comes from the interaction
The interaction Leads to reciprocation
The reciprocation causes to reflection
The reflection turns into realization

The realization recalls his obligation
The obligation gives a right solution
The solution will become liberation
The liberation satisfies population

The population gives standing ovation
The ovation reverberates in a nation
The nation salutes, giving veneration
The veneration is proper justification

26. Parents are not servants

Children should be taught few principles
to grow better and to live happily always
They should know, mothers aren't maids
They should know, fathers aren't servants

Teach them, "How to be independent?"
Then only, they will learn to compete
Preach them, "Grattitude is important"
Then they will become very confident

Inculcate good hobbies among them
as hobbies form to view with optimism
Educate them, "Learn with enthusiasm"
as education will only transform them

27. Love starts from attraction

People say, "Love is just attraction"
I feel, "Love starts from attraction"
The attraction turns into affection
The affection becomes adoration

Falling in love is not planned one
It will just happen at any situation
It is a disease and has no medicine
It won't die, resumes even in heaven

Love is a bittersweet experience
A lover needs a lot of patience
It teaches to show only kindness
It has more sadness, less happiness

28. A way to progress

No dream is great activity for us
Perseverance is a way to progress
Obstacles are common for humans
Dropping down will bring distress

Rigorous efforts will give success
Lying dormantly makes lazy beings
Active mind will achieve many things
Self-motivation shuns from failures

Frivolousness gives less results
Our dream should act as stimulus
Otherwise our life will in crisis
Success is overcoming challenges

29. A spiritual leader

Ramakrishna Paramahamsa was a spiritual leader
He devoted his life to goddess Kali in Dakshineshwar
He was Hindu, Christian and Muslim follower
Paramahamsa found the same god at everywhere

He experienced spiritual wonders at the age of tender
He assimilated whole knowledge of the nature
He said, "Jal, Paani and water are very similar"
He said, "There is no religion for pitcher and water"

For many disciples, he became a great teacher
The school later turned into Ramakrishna order
Swami Vivekanada made his ideas popular
Today, his ideas are trained in every nook and corner

30. The warrior

To this king, "do or die" is not the maxim
Stepping back and winning is aphorism
He was cultured, saw his mother in a lady
He is the Indian king, Chatrapthi Shivaji

At tender age, he had to hold the sword
So Shivaji became the warrior & legend
He was the king, had religious tolerance
He had banned the anti-social elements

Shivaji had introduced the Guerilla war
He made known multi usage of water
Chatrapathi protected our mother land
And he tried save the culture and creed

31. Social justice

Social justice is the distribution of privileges
It tells the people to fulfil their societal roles
It assigns the rights and duties to the individuals
And social justice is one of the humas' virtues

Social justice makes the society harmonious
Politicians are taking it in various dimensions
They are involving the communities in the politics
With it, the progress will be like a snail's pace

Social justice has to meet the poor's needs
And it has to take care of the human rights
Throw away the bad beliefs and practices
Harness to the new developmental policies

32. Our tongue in vogue

Mother tongue is always in vogue
Other tongue is always in vague
Expression in own tongue is simple
Expression in other tongue is typical

Globalization reduced usage of Telugu
But speaking Telugu is not grotesque
Now it is the time to rescue Telugu
Telugu language always has its value

Of all languages, Telugu is the sweetest
So it is called as, "Italian of the east"
Own tongue overcomes miscommunication
Regional languages develop their nation

33. W/o Gandhi

There is a woman behind every successful man
To this, Mahatma Gandhi was not exception
As a wife to Gandhi, she was an inspiration
But bout her, people were very little known

Like Gandhi, Katsurba was also a freedom fighter
In his movements, she was an active volunteer
She inspired many local women as a philosopher
She taught them to keep their places cleaner

She was on the fast when Gandhi was in jail
She didn't stop it even She had become fragile
Her unprecedented support is recalled by all
Her birthday is now safe motherhood day of national

34. Prevention from peril

Peace is the permanent pacification
Feuds will fail to keep us in federation
Peace is pleasant, war is the worst
So avoid fights to appease the heart

Good understanding leads to peace
Miscommunication makes a lot of noise
Understanding comes with empathy
Communication comes with interactivity

Bombs may petrify people's survival
Guns may terrify the innocent people
And other weapons may great turmoil
Peace prevents the people from peril

35. My rustic students

My students are very rustic
They are brilliant and terrific
They hail from the villages
But their talent is marvellous

My students' heart is genuine
They are appreciated by everyone
They may a step back in studies
But they have excellent life skills

My students are my favorite
To them I am only the favorite
Their love is very unconditional
I am very lucky to have such pupil

36. A challenging day

Reporting the school in the morning
Since then, the day is very challenging
There will be myriad duties to perform
The duty is not permitted to classroom

Rest room, dining room, dormitory room
All the rooms may like me to maximum
I am stupefied, why not the staff room?
Later I knew, I have addendum with them

One tells that he is beaten by someone
One says that there is no water in latrine
A parent tells why there is a hole in den
A teacher enquires if the bell has rung

37. A sudden war

The world is upset with Russia's invasion
It is Russia's unpardonable incursion
Tension prevailed in the small Ukraine
In NATO countries, tension is clearly seen

Everyone is stupefied with sudden war
The world never expected this seizure
The U.S.A is playing the role of curator
Many war deaths are grown at the border

NATO has a penchant for expansionism
Russia has a severe fear and skepticism
In between these, Ukraine became victim
It is begging the question about humanism

38. Our view

Our view is based on the people we depend
If we depend on our parents, life will be good
If we live independently, life will be not so bad
If we take responsibility, life will be perturbed

Mother's lap is the safest place in the world
Father's shoulder is the highest peak in the world
Sister's company is the most entertaining episode
Brother's caring is the cutest and candid bond

Friend's help in the emergency is much touched
Colleague's counsel is the best solution indeed
Lover's unconditional love is the purest mood
Spouse's sacrifice is the most valuable fund

39. Small country-brave leader

Zelenskyy is now an address for leadership
He has not given up hope in the hardship
In emergency, "Leaders flee to safe nation"
But brave Zelenskyy said, "I need ammunition"

As a comedian, he entertained his people
As a president, he ruled as the role model
As a human, he has stolen people's hearts
As a soldier, he tried to instilled confidence

Zelenskyy is the sole leader in the world
He has stood strong even Russia invaded
Insidious firing didn't tremble this leader
Whole world stupefied seeing his valour

40. Outstanding Raman

C.V. Raman might not be physically strong
But, in science, Raman was outstanding
To him, books were like his close friends
And he was inspired by the great minds

Raman was famous for original thinking
In light waves subject, he was very strong
Then there were no laboratories in India
But his interest in science was not trivia

He did research on the sounds and light
His wisdom discovered Raman's effect
For this, he was awarded with Nobel Prize
That is why, the Indians always idealize

41. Shiva

On Mahashivarathri, Lord Shiva married Parvathi
The Hindus celebrate this festival annually grandly
On this day, Shiva performs cosmic dance beautifully
This is a wonderful day for the people to self study

Festival gives a chance to defeat stupidity in life
Fasting brings peace to the mind and keep it safe
Meditation prevents soul, doing the things of mischief
Multiple benefits, one gets and stays always relief

Shivarathri significantly symbolizes spiritual soul
Shiva lives everywhere in cosmos, even in our soul
Shivarathri is a good chance to introspect our soul
Shiva is the god who protects us with his lively soul

42. A neem tree

The neem tree is the optimism
for the gents staff of T.M.R.S
During leisure they come from
classes to refresh themselves

Some come to talk on phones
Some come to talk the gossips
For few it is the resting place
For few it is the privacy space

It's good place for nature's call
and to be free from foul smell
Thus Neem tree is memorable
for the staff of college & school

43. The queen of sciences

Maths isn't just counting numbers
It is measurement of many things
It is also proposing the questions
And it is language of the universe

It teaches arithmetical operations
One can apply it to real life events
And it is the spontaneity of ideas
So it's called, the queen of sciences

Maths is now the subject of essence
Without it there will be no progress
All of us should give the importance
because Maths is lifetime's process

44. The sun is our hope

The morning sun is people's hope
The full moon may fulfil the hope
Our hopes are like hops of a rabbit
The binkies of kit are fun to look at

Our hopes are also very amusing
until we come into reality of the life
The sun is nice but after its setting
the moon keeps our hopes in safe

Every day, we carry lots of emotions
The emotions change our moods
Wake up early and look at the sun
to call it the day with a lot of fun

45. A stepping stone

Falling down is a stepping stone
Failure leads to the progress
Humiliation becomes appreciation
Disgrace turns into the greatness

Only thing you need is self-restraint
Strive hard without waiting for upshot
Success is the internal contentment
Failure is soothing the soul and heart

Plant becomes extinct in the ground
Tree falls down but grows with seed
Live and lead your life with optimism
Your hard work should be a paradigm

46. A throwback

2021 gave away many throwbacks
It retained our feelings and fantasies
It made us to recall fears and feuds
It preserved our surprises and sadness

The year was not like any other year
The Covid's fear prevailed altogether
The panic regularly took to the doctor
Thus the peace became the warrior

2022 deletes jealous, keeps us in jolly
It makes us with awe, removes agony
The year tells us to be with empathy
Lastly it keeps us happy and healthy

47. Sacred Sankranti

Sankranti is the harvest festival
The festival reunites all the people
Sons-in-law make festival colourful
Chicken bets, Rangolis are special

The sun transits into Capricorn
People learn the success lesson
Haridasu comes and purifies sin
A decorated bull will entertain

Tasty pastry dishes make it grand
Flying kites gives happiness to child
Bhogi sends out the things of old
Sankranti fills optimism in the world

48. Fasting is fabulous

Fasting means living near to the god
It isn't being without eating the food
Soul is experienced, not expressed
It is only thing that can't be spittled

Ekadasi means eleven human senses
It is knotting the soul and the senses
Ekadasi fasting is knowing life's truth
Life is, knowing the secret behind myth

Ekadasi is the inner power of Vishnu
The power had killed Mura, a demon
So Murari name was given to Vishnu
North door is a symbol inner shrine

49. Bhogi- glory

Bhogi is the time for leading luxurious life
By this time harvests are yielded and sold
The farmers get food and money by festive
It is the result of farmers' labour in the field

On this day, people worship rainy god, Indra
They will get salvation in the form of Karma
The real happiness is getting the salvation
The last day in winter solstice is celebration

Rangolis are for protecting from the insects
Jujubes are for the children's bright future
Bonfire is for sending away the inner evils
Bhogi is preparaing for seasonal changes

50. The root cause of ego

Insecurity is the root cause of ego
Ego kills confidence and will power
It makes people to live with sorrow
Not the power, it makes them lower

People with ego lose relationships
Dominance attitude brings failures
The winner transforms into whiner
Fantastic person becomes fantasizer

Learn to appreciate the achievers
Help the needy, with selflessness
Be ready to accept the criticisms
Should pactice of being openness

51. Live in India

Our country has all kinds of resources
It is no use of going to other countries
Study and work hard in the mother land
Losing lives in unknown country is so sad

You may go for education or employment
Excelling in the life is also very important
But you can nourish in your own country
Indirectly, you can fulfil your responsibility

It is sad to hear the demise of our student
Dying in Ukraine war is very unfortunate
I have a thought if he has studied in India
He would have lived without any phobia

52. Misunderstanding

Misunderstanding is the communication gap
Miss understanding makes the best relationship
Mrs understanding has only the dictatorship
Mrs understanding will develop good friendship

Assumption is the main reason for misunderstanding
Communication compromises Miss understanding
Hallucination confuses Mrs understanding
Relaxation is the solution for Mr understanding

Misunderstanding leads to so many problems
Miss understanding keeps us in happiness
Mrs understanding always ducks in sadness
Mr understanding never compromises in all situations

53. Brutal war

Renouncing war after genocide is brutal
History recalls these incidents of critical
Emperor Ashoka realized in Kalinga battle
Heap of the dead bodies changed his soul

George Bush did the same during Iraq war
Didn't Putin witness the history before?
This is the time to strive for tranguil sphere
Otherwise these genocides will reoccur

In those days, the invaders were praised
In these days, the pacifists are admired
The blunders should be kept as a record
History teaches to be united not to divide

54. Lovely loyal love

You are my lovely loyal love
I am your laudable lifetime lover
Our love surely lasts luminously
Listen my lady! Lifelong I love you

Please pardon me if I hurt you
Accept me with your humble heart
I can give up anything except you
I won't live without lying in your heart

Don't say, these are movie dialogues
They are the reflection of lovers' feelings
If not you, who will understand me
It is you who knew me greatly

55. Who will recognize us?

We are the women labourers
We want maternity leaves
We need creche facilities
We expect high daily wages

We long for good job conditions
We want to beat our poorness
We need child care solutions
We expect many health benefits

We need more anganwadi centers
We expect many welfare schemes
We long for affordable services
We want facilities as literate ladies

56. The first woman teacher

Savithri Bhai Pule was the first woman teacher
Besides that, she was also feminist and worker
Malala was born in form her before independence
Like Malala, she had studied in horrendous situations

It is true, those want to do good will be treated as bad
From society, they will be isolated and banished
The humiliations didn't let Savithri Bhai Phule down
Her will power to do good to the poor made her queen

She filled hope in the women by erasing social atrocities
She started a school for the depressed communities
Even the Britishers recognized her great services
She still remained as an icon for women and girls

57. Big brain

Albert Einstein was the greatest physicist
For quantum mechanics, he is the best
His formula from relativity is very famous
He imparted many contributions to physics

He says, " Geniusness is based on ability"
People become genius if they've creativity
If you repeat the same thing, it is insanity
If you take difficulty, you'll get opportunity

Alber Einstein was known of his humility
His simplicity made him great personality
He received Nobel Prize for his services
Even today, Einstein is the most genius

58. Social media

Social media is affecting the democracy
The parties on the platform, gaining popularity
Social media is supporting one to earn money
It is illegally interfering in electoral policy

It is giving priority to those who are in the power
The companies are giving ad offers on lower
The leader became a business man, not ruler
The youth is being misled by looking at ads' manner

Money is becoming important in the democracy
For the parties misleading has become very easy
If it continues there will be no societal harmony
Putting an end to this system benefits democracy

59. Colourful festival

Holi is the beautiful festival
Each colour plays a vital role
Red is for fashion and royal
Yellow is for mirth and ideal

All the days won't be equal
Some days are so colourful
Some days are very dull
And some days are normal

Holi is good's victory over evil
The god protects from the devil
All should celebrate with dil
Holi is the happiest festival

60. Forest day

The role of forests in humans' life is conspicuous
Forests provide everything to animals and humans
So it is very important to create awareness
Forest day celebration recalls the efforts of nations

Forests are the source of sustainable development
Expanding the forests' area is very important
Without forests, biodiversity is completely lost
Protecting them is in the hands of the government

The forests will prevent the violent activities
Abundant resources will keep people in peace
Apart from NGOs, everyone should strive to increase
Forests are like seeing gods, they always bless

61. Sound of soul

Poetry is the resonance of the conscience
It is only the perfect medium to express
The people may not understand one's feelings
Poetry intervenes and tells about their opinions

Story beats around the bush for a simple thing
Poetry briefs even the history without prolong
Sometimes story, drama may be disappointing
But poetry is always amusing and amazing

The power of torrent is known to the swimmer
The power of poetry is only known to poet and reader
Poetry primarily is for pleasure and soul purifier
Poetry paints to the feelings and uncover the fervour

62. Wonderful water

Water is the wonderful creation by god
Without water, way of life becomes odd
Worth of water has to be known to the world
Whatever, water is vital or whole life will end

We can live without love, not without water
Water drop is soul soother and life saver
Water in any form will be an entertainer
Waterfall is the most thrilling and grandeur

Warmth of the sun in the winter is beautiful
Water in the warm weather is so delightful
Water might be ambrosia, drunk by the angel
Water is the best medicine so have it plentiful

63. Don't tense

Learn the tenses without much tense
If you are tensed, tenses'll distress us
There are only three princiapl tenses
Present Tense, Future and past tense

Each tense is divided into four tenses
They are the Simple and Continuous
The next are Perfect, Perfect Continuous
Each tense has its structure and uses

Simple tense expresses general truths
In continuous, the action is in progress
In Perfect tense, the action completes
Perfect continous, repeated activities

64. Eye peel

Indian Premier League is a popular game
It became famous as it has mixed team
The creative thought won even criticism
On social media, it has full following game

The players have full of freedom in game
Every ball thrills the audience in stadium
The stadium is not only one medium
The thrilling prevails on every platform

It is not based on team, individual fame
To the players, it gets money and name
The batters Dhoni, Gayle, Rohit are some
The bowlers are Jaddu, Bhumra Boom

65. Great granny

She always gives money without asking
She fills empty stomach by feeding
She tells moral stories while sleeping
She is the one who shows her fondling

Granny is the person, symbol of loving
She is more than mother, makes frosting
No one beats grand mother in caring
That is why granny is always amazing

Granny is the encyclopedia for learning
She shows right path during misleading
Commanding at the same time soothing
She turns heartbreaking into comforting

66. Entertainer

Visiting waterfall brings euphoria
Waterfall will take you to Utopia
Birds entertain you on the way
Animals sate you with their play

The pavements test your ability
Your gasping tells to stay healthy
Water view reminds to be happy
There, you feel all are temporary

The nature says to forget the past
Small island awakes inactive heart
It tells to take of clothes, swim in it
Savouring in it is the most important

67. Tower of love

Eiffel tower is the wonder of the world
French revolution inspired and it bred
Later the tower became a symbol of love
For the couple, it is becoming supportive

The tower was built by Gustave Eiffel
The main material used, was metal
It is made of metal but looks natural
That is why, Eiffel is a wonder of visual

Some places become faded and old
Eiffel tower's view never gets bored
The tower is not just a pretty place
Eiffel is a jewel to Paris and France

68. Telugu new year

Ugadi festival is the telugu new year
It brings new aspiration and desire
Life is a blend of tears and laughter
Ugadi tells about life as a philosopher

Sweet is tasty but not good for health
Bitter isn't tasty but it's the real wealth
Ugadi ceases the struggles and dearth
People with a lot of zeal, reaches zenith

When nature blooms, Ugadi happens
When Ugadi comes, happiness starts
When happiness stops, Ugadi blesses
When Ugadi blesses, the nature thrills

69. Language and love

Asku in Turkish and amor in Spanish
Lamour in French and love in English
Ast in Icelandic and Ishq in Arabic
Words are different but love is a magic

Marriage ends with mutual divorce
Relationship ends by deleting memories
True love takes birth but it never ends
To end love, society has no legal process

In true love, feelings always haunt
Even one wants to forgo it, they can't
Physical body may die but love won't
Till today, true love didn't die, it is a ghost

70. Health is not wealth

Health is actually more than the wealth
Wealth is not so important for existence
Existence is not possible without health
Wealth gives luxury but health gives bliss

Wealth brings you reputation and money
Health gets you good friends and family
If you're wealthy, you'll be hope to anybody
If you're healthy, to thyself, thou are worthy

Wealth is just a matter of land and gold
Health is having proper flesh and blood
Being wealthy, you may have bright future
Being healthy, you will be the right creature

71. National song

Indian national song is Vandemataram
The limpid lyrics were written by Bankim
Vandemataram evoked national patriotism
The song praises mother India's freedom

Vandemataram describes Indians' dream
It reiterates the country's strength, wisdom
It retells India's esteem, beauty and charm
It portrays Indias' power all over the realm

The song is a symbol of country's custom
It is a song of sovereign, sung with rhythm
It is a song of India's soul, praised heroism
The song ever blooms like chrysanthemum

72. Good friday

Crucifixion was the transgression
Humiliation became succession
Resurrection brought exhilaration
It became a good commemoration

A bad friday became a good friday
Jesus's sacrifice made it a holy day
So governments declared holiday
For the Christians, it is a great day

It is a day of conquering humanity
Calvary is the spot for the almighty
Here, the Christians perform Liturgy
Jesus Christ's soul is the immortality

73. I am a mobile phone

I am the mostly used mobile phone
Men invented me for commutation
But my work is to work for commotion
Like nuclear is used in atom weapon

Almost I have all the good features
But people use them for negatives
People can lock me for their purpose
As a result, the relationship spoils

I can connect the two different souls
I can disconnect with my strategies
I can create people as bad characters
I can become addiction in their lives

74. Easter

Easter is the resurrection Sunday
To the Christians, it is a joyful day
Jesus returned to life, on this day
His sacrifice filled mirth and gay

Hope is the wonderful blessing
If hope is truth, it will be amazing
People are lazy at least for hoping
Hope lies in shell, try for breaking

Easter tells people will never die
Their virtue lives, it is always high
Love is a thing, lies above the sky
The virtue and love are the lullaby

75. Lovely life

Life will be lovely with laughter and lull
Life will be lifeless with no goal and grail
See that there'll be no lackluster and banal
Spend at favorite place and be comfortable

Build more memories then it'll be beautiful
Have whatever you want to have and LOL
Go out for a movie, watch it with delightful
Have wine with crunchy bites of tasteful

Make a day as special and rest on laurel
Take a sound sleep as sleep is healthful
Fight with siblings as it is quite natural
Don't waste time without doing above all

76. Peace of mind

Beauty is only not important thing in life
Peace of mind adds beauty to the life
To be peaceful, one needs some relief
Otherwise, the life will be full of stuff

Beauty may attract the human beings
The attraction brings so many problems
The problems make the life hideous
If life is ugly, what'll be the use of face?

So, stop boasting about one's beauty
Beauty is not property, it's just identity
Beauty is like sunset, it vanishes slowly
Basic needs make us happy, not beauty

77. A square meal

Nobody knows the hard work of a workman
He works day and night and in rain or shine
For some people, the life is so comfortable
For some people, the life is very miserable

A swimmer knows the strength of a stream
A watcher enjoys, not knowing his problem
A labourer leads the life with much effort
A white collar employee leads with affluent

Just for a square meal, a labourer may die
With dyspeptic meal, a fat cat joins the sky
Life is tough, a layman tries to make it easy
Life is easy but a rich man makes it ugly

78. Bye bye

Farewell is not sending off or saying bye bye
Keeping the loved ones in heart until we die
Farewell is the reminiscence of past memories
Living by recalling them is a wonderful experience

The sunset calls it a day but looks beautiful
Sometimes, the ending of something is ideal
Bride is bidden farewell with the flow of tears
But parents' aim is to send off their daughters

A soldier goes to warfare to protect the country
Even the death is not the final, it is immortality
Every ending in the life is for a new beginning
So farewell is not ending, it's for developing

79. Master blaster

He grew from master Sachin to master blaster
He rose from Galli cricketer to international cricketer
There weren't any accolades that he hadn't won
There weren't any records the cricketers could attain

Sachin Tendulkar is not a name, it's a cricket brand
That is why, cricket lovers treat him as cricket God
It isn't exaggeration that none can beat his record
This versatile cricketer is kind, modest and determined

In Indian Cricket history, Sachin occupies lion's share
With his play, Everybody became a cricket lover
He is a former player but his charisma died down
His qualities made him world favourite sports person

80. No one is same

No two people are the same in total
The earth is the commonality for all
Property doesn't mean money or gold
In future, property means a safe world

The earth has hundred crores of history
Ages back, it was pristine, pure, pretty
In the recent years, it was deteriorated
Now there is no hope for the mankind

The only thing we do is, rehabilating it
Otherwise, living beings turn into dirt
Don't feel our death is far in the future
If we don't realize, we can't see nature

81. Tortoise wins

A boy walks like a tortoise while going to school
He leaps like a rabbit while going to domicile
You might know the tale of a tortoise and a rabbit
Tortoise walks slow but wins eventually in the bet

Home is a safer and comfortable place to anyone
School maybe tedious place but it makes you win
The thing which gets you happiness, ends with grief
The thing which gets you grief, keeps you safe in life

So every student should feel school is to be home to win
You'll know the value of shade if you stand in sunshine
School is sunshine, keeps you hot but gives light
Home is shade, you may loll but you need support

82. Accuracy

Standing on one's word is different
Speaking that one can do is different
The first one is absolutely, honesty
The second one is known as philosophy

Doing what one tells is different
Telling what one does is different
The first one is called as commitment
The second one is truly transparent

Winning over the others is different
Winning the hearts of others is different
The first one is a winning practice
The second one is known as essence

Going far ignoring the things is different
Knowing how far one has to go is different

The first one is known as exciting event
The second one is known as judgment

83. Too much is nonsense

It's true, too much is nonsense
Too much eating makes obese
Too much dieting causes risks
Too much talking leads to dins

Too much thinking leads to stress
Too much reading exhausts
Too much arguments- breakups
Too much love- cross boundaries

Too much medicine-heavy dose
Too much imagination suffers
Too much doubting relation spoils
Too much goodness brings struggles

84. Materialistic mind

Our mind diverts when we do chanting
Our mind focuses while money counting
We don't listen while others are speaking
We feel bitter, why are others not listening?

Our heart feels sad, when it is hurt
Our heart feels happy, when we hurt
We always talk about the others a lot
We hardly talk about ourselves a bit

Our eyes shed tears when they are sad
Our eyes are reason for others' bad mood
We want to see only bad even there's good
We don't want to be seen our fault by God

85. Anger is enemy

We shouldn't reciprocate in anger
Others may try to keep us bother
Try to be in peace and be healthier
Others can't feed us except differ

Abuses are like unaccepted gifts
If you accept, it will be with us
If you don't, it will be with givers
Even Budha received the abuses

With this, Budha became a lord
And inspired so many in the world
No one can harm us if we are good
Finally believe in be good, do good

86. Krishna Leelas

Krishna leelas are never understood
His wit has a purpose but looks bad
He teaches, how to control our mind?
He is the hidden power for humankind

We blame Krishna for our troubles
Krishna always tests our patience
But his tests have a special purpose
If we overcome, life will be gorgeous

Krishna's color teaches many things
He looks blue but he is glamorous
Struggles are dark but they shine us
Believing in him is blessing in disguise

87. No bonding only building

Food has more value than affection
Money has more value than adoration
Building has more value than bonding
Loving has more value than enduring

External things always attract people
No one understands, what is in soul?
Success is important, not the potential
Material is greater, not the spiritual

If one satisfies ego, good they'll become
To win, they behave without decorum
Life will be beautiful If you avoid them
But avoiding them is a very big problem

88. Dad's mothers

To father, daughter is an apple of eye
His caring towards her is above the sky
Dads make stand their daughters high
For them, Daring Dads will be with sigh

Daughters always recall dads' mothers
That is why, the daughters are mothers
With daughters, don dads become dudes
They teach to be down to earth to dads

Daughters' hearts are softer than petals
Their words are sweeter than the songs
Their presence fills the home with lights
Their birthdays are greater than festivals

89. Literature's labourer

I am a labourer of English literature
In the literature, I am a small creature
Spending time for it is my expenditure
Writing is my pleasure and it's my future

My mind does hardwork as a labourer
Labourer sprinkles sweat even in winter
My mind won't allow me to enjoy weather
My mind is on is like a duty of chevalier

I always do labour for the best outcome
Labourer toils hard and he eats on time
My mind is hungry, it wants only wisdom
I proudly say, I am a labourer of my poem

90. Hard work

Honest hard work is always the heaven
Hurdles, humans face are the common
Harness to hard work to make it happen
Hunt daily in habitat as if you're aborigine

Hero changes horrible into harmonious
Heroic hard work removes all the hurdles
Hide the negatives and have confidence
Hard work is a herb, it cures life's illness

Hard work is like a harp, produces music
Have hope on the process to be prolific
Heap hath history, public makes it ironic
Hard work never goes waste, it's a logic

91. Combats' lessons

Consciousness comes from combats
Culture is formed from the life styles
Protecting it is the duty of everybody's
Polluting it, leads to historical mistakes

Real beauty lies in culture of a country
Different lifestyles will teach us many
We can find strife if you look at history
Jesus, Allah, Ram fought for humanity

Let's not shun our culture and society
Without it, our lives will be bad and ugly
Hesitation will give us only difficulty
Fighting spirit will change us totally

92. Success is a process

Don't care jeers, ridicules, mockeries
If you care, the success won't be yours
Turn low estimation into the praises
Success is a process, it has no secrets

Any process will be looked too tedious
Look movie shooting, it is monotonous
Watch it as a movie, it'll be tremendous
It is same with cooking and all others

Abraham Lincoln is regarded as famous
He was successful after myriad failures
After success, no one cares the process
But during the process, only the sneers

93. Peg and drug

Peg, drug, smoking are fascinating
If you use them, life'll be appalling
The body parts slowly stop working
The mental health will be decreasing

Students will drop from their studies
Employees will lose their good jobs
Youth's career will have no hopes
Relationships will end with breakups

To prevent, peg, drug and smoking
Try to inculcate the hobby of reading
Playing games will be so entertaining
So no peg or drug, stay back in the rug

94. Be the change

Change is the necessity for the society
Selfishness makes the society dirty
Accountability makes it so healthy
Change isn't a noun, a verb, our duty

Politicians are playing with democracy
Hunting for positions is now diplomacy
There is more publicity, less practicality
No spirit of majority, currency is priority

The women still remained in the slavery
Majority of the people are living in poverty
Unemployment is a curse to the country
So change is imperative for the society

95. Ballot vs wallet

Ballot vote is greater than wallet
An electorate elects their favorite
Vote is potent, do not misuse it
It's unfortunate, few are selling it

Everyone is eligible to cast vote
Some are enthusiastic about it
Some have no awareness of it
The problem is with the illiterate

Vote can change country's fate
In voting, all should participate
Vote forms a good government
That government will legislate

96. Plastic covers

Trees are the home for birds, animals
The statement used to be said once
Now, plastic bags replaced the animals
How eccentric! The people's follies

"Don't use plastic bags" a good saying
Ok, they are using as laws aren't working
Don't they know where to throw? Irritating
Do they dump them on trees? Disgusting

Environment's beauty is in trees, water
Plastic bags are the bandages of sufferer
They are like the smears on a white paper
Nature became nasty with plastic cover

97. Mother is everything

Mother is model of virtue and good
Her all acts make the children proud
She cooks food and tells only good
She is god, guard, kind and unbiased

Imagine no mother, life is awkward
All the deadly evils prevail in the world
Mother is root cause of the humankind
So the greatest blessing is motherhood

Mother is a role model for every child
Everyone is blessed as she is living god
She needs children's progress, not gold
She takes care of everything till her end

98. Growth is for bad

Growth in the life is only for shrinking
Day by day, the cost of living is growing
People's thirst for luxury is developing
On the other hand, pollution is thriving

What not, almost all things are at hike
Now GDP abbreviation turned as joke
GDP means Gas, diesel and Petrol's hike
People are intolerant, they started strike

But what about humans' span of life?
It has dropped to fifty but not wildlife
So know, growth in the life is unsafe
Live your life fully, not fifty, a midlife

99. Don't believe in luck factor

If you believe in luck, you will be lazy
If you work hard, you will be so lucky
Luck may not bring success, luxury
Hard work definitely make you happy

Don't sit idle even you've innate talent
Talent may be gift, hard work is asset
Anything comes to life only if we use it
In the same way with the skill and talent

An ability to think is a sign of success
Put it into practice to become winners
So just stop keeping your fingers cross
Wake up and start working for progress

100. No end for evils

I think there will be no end for poverty
Unable to eradicate it, we say "destiny"
Society has high unemployment rate
But we say there is lot of requirement

There are plenty of acts on child labour
But no law is favour, it takes as humour
Still child marriage is the most savage
The damage it created is only disparage

The dowry system now became fashion
Giving dowry is a status and competition
Caste feeling is beating the love feeling
Falling in love is based on money earning

101. Beautiful earth

She was beautiful in the universe
She is not gorgeous and glorious
Her skin is applied with chemicals
So she is ravaged by acne, pimples

Her jewels were trees and forests
They are robbed by her dear kids
Her long hair is rivers and waterfalls
They are dried by her kids' activities

Her smile is lopsided with sadness
Her inner peace is welfare of species
Peace is lost with their disappearance
Hoping for recuperate of her cuteness